Investing in
TREASURY
BILLS

M. J. Abadie

LONGMEADOW
P R E S S

My thanks to Allen Erdheim, M.B.A., for generously sharing his expertise and for preparation of the graph materials.

Cover design by Nancy Sabato

Interior design by Richard Oriolo

Library of Congress Cataloging-in-Publication Data

Abadie, M. J.
   No nonsense financial guide to investing in treasury bills / by M.J. Abadie.—1st ed.
     p.   cm. — (No nonsense financial guides)
   ISBN: 0-681-41793-5
   1. Treasury bills—United States. 2. Investments—United States. I. Title. II. Series
HG4936.A2   1992
332.63′232—dc20   92—26770
                                CIP

Printed in United States of America

First Edition

0 9 8 7 6 5 4 3 2 1

Contents

What Are Treasury Securities?

Backed up by the full faith and protection of the U.S. Government, Treasury securities, often called "Treasuries," are a sound and low-risk investment. They can be part of a wisely chosen varied portfolio, the base of your investment *pyramid*. An investment pyramid is a graphic way of depicting the division of your investments into various categories. These categories are, in descending order:

1. *Aggressive Growth*—Stocks, Bonds, and Funds
2. *Investment Growth*—Mutual Funds and Stocks
3. *Safety and High Return*—Corporate and Municipal Bonds, Treasury Notes and Bonds, and Fixed Income Funds
4. *Safety and Liquidity*—Treasury bills, CDs, Money Market Funds, Savings Accounts

Investment Pyramid

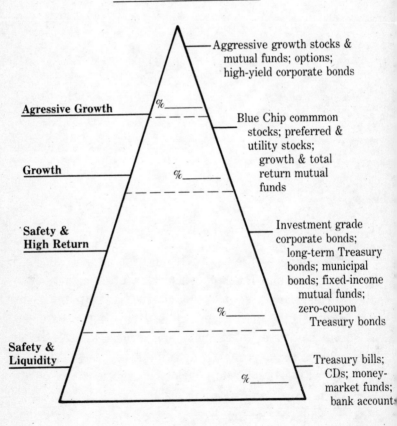

Aggressive Growth

Growth

Safety & High Return

Safety & Liquidity

%_____

%_____

%_____

%_____

Aggressive growth stocks & mutual funds; options; high-yield corporate bonds

Blue Chip commmon stocks; preferred & utility stocks; growth & total return mutual funds

Investment grade corporate bonds; long-term Treasury bonds; municipal bonds; fixed-income mutual funds; zero-coupon Treasury bonds

Treasury bills; CDs; money-market funds; bank accounts

What Are Treasury Securities?

Many financial advisors suggest that—depending on your age and your financial goals—you invest anywhere from 10 to 80 percent of your funds in the "base" of your investment pyramid, categories 3 and 4. The bottom of the pyramid base includes Treasury bills, the ultimate investment in terms of safety and liquidity. The second segment of the base includes other Treasury securities, such as Treasury notes and bonds.

Who Issues Treasury Securitites?

Treasury securities are issued by the United States Department of the Treasury through its system of Federal Reserve banks (Treasury Direct) and through other financial institutions, such as commercial banks and securities dealers/brokers.

Why Does the Government Issue Treasury Securities?

The U.S. Government issues its Treasury securities in order to *borrow money from you, the investor.*

We are all familiar with the huge federal budget deficit and the problems it causes. It is because of this deficit, which has been rising at an alarming rate over the years, that the government must borrow money. Taxes may have once paid for all the Government's expenses, but today there is a big gap in Government's revenue and its financial obligations. And so the

Government *borrows* from investors—individuals and institutions.

Treasury securities are in reality *debt securities*. They are known as debt securities because they are the means by which the Government acquires its debt.

In order to borrow on such a large scale, the Government uses its ability to issue Treasury securities. That is to say, the Government offers to *sell* its debt securities to the investor. It does not matter if the potential investor is an individual with a small amount of money or a corporation or financial institution with billions of dollars to invest.

When you buy a Treasury security you are, in point of fact, *loaning* the Government your money, just as a bank loans you money when you buy a house. And, just as a bank charges you interest on the money you borrow, the Government must pay interest on the money it borrows. As a buyer of Treasury securities, you are a lender to the United States Government. The "security" is the promise of the Government to pay off its debt to you when the bill or bond matures (comes due). It is also the guarantee to pay the specified interest rate.

Thus the term *security* indicates that this is a secure investment. And it is. Treasury securities are backed by the full faith and power of the United States of America.

Who Buys Treasury Securities?

Anyone can buy Treasury securities.

Lots of "little people" buy them. Ask around and

you will probably find people you know who own Treasury securities.

Investors large and small, private and institutional, are purchasers of Treasury securities, which are much admired for their flexibility as well as safety.

Individual investors buy Treasury securities for their personal portfolios.

Financial institutions buy Treasury securities for their own and their clients' portfolios.

Managers of mutual funds and pension funds buy Treasury securities as an investment vehicle for their funds.

Professional investors buy Treasury bills as a means of short-term investments.

Foreigners buy Treasury securities. In fact, foreigners are particularly happy to invest in U.S. Treasury securities because of the stability of our government. Many foreigners view us as being the most stable and secure country in the world. In the great rush of foreign capital to the United States in recent years, a great deal of investment has been going into Treasury securities. This is an indication of the general esteem of the United States in the eyes of the world. And many of these foreign investors are very big investors indeed—they have millions of dollars in cash, making the market for U.S. Treasury securities one of the largest in the world.

The nice thing is that you can play a part in his good thing, too. You don't have to be a billionaire oil sheik to invest in your government. The ordinary citizen is not only invited, he is actively solicited to invest his money in his own country's future.

And because of the popularity of this investment tool, an investor can rest assured that there is a place to buy and sell Treasury securities whenever he or she desires.

Different Types of Treasury Securities

Treasury Bills are short-term obligations of the U.S. Treasury. They are issued with a three-, six-, and twelve-month maturity period. The *minimum* purchase for a Treasury bill is $10,000; after that initial amount, you can buy in increments of $5,000.

Treasury Notes are a medium-term obligation of the U.S. Treasury. They are issued with maturity dates from two to ten years. Investment amount is in $1,000 or $5,000 denominations. Interest on these longer-term notes is paid every six months.

Treasury Bonds are a long-term obligation of the U.S. Treasury. They are issued with maturity dates of over ten years. Except for the longer maturity period, they are similar to Treasury notes.

Zero-Coupon Treasuries (sometimes called *STRIPS*) are Treasury notes and bonds that are sold at a discount. Unlike regular Treasury notes and bonds, which pay interest semiannually, zero-coupon Treasuries pay their interest in one lump sum at maturity (one to 30 years). The interest, however, is *compounded semiannually*, which means that an initial investment can show considerable growth over time. Zero-coupons are often favored for tax-deferred accounts.

6

This table will help you to compare the three types of Treasury securities:

	Bills	Notes	Bonds
Maturities at Issuance	3, 6 mo, 1 yr.	2, 3, 4, 5, & 10 yr.	30 years
Minimum Denomination	$10,000	2 & 3 yr.— $5,000 4–10 yr.— $1,000	$1,000
Incremental Investments	$5,000	2 & 3 yr.— $5,000 4–10 yr.— $1,000	$1,000
Interest Payments	Treasury bills are issued at a discount to face value. The return to the investor is the difference between the purchase price and face value.	Semi-annually—	Semiannually
Income Tax Treatment		Treasury securities are exempt from state and local income taxes but subject to federal income taxes.	
Guarantee		Timely payment of interest and principal on all Treasury securities is guaranteed by the full faith and credit of the U.S.A.	

Purpose of a Treasury Bill

Unlike Treasury notes and bonds, the Treasury bill is a short-term investment. It offers the large or small investor (or lender) a convenient place to park money for a short time, with maximum safety and liquidity (or convertibility into cash).

In order to accomplish its necessary borrowing, attracting the large scale of funds it requires, the U.S. must offer many types of investment opportunities. It must also compete in the open market with other types of investments, such as stocks and bonds. The Government knows there are many investors with considerable amounts of cash—up in the billions of dollars in the case of some foreign interests—who don't want to put these funds into long-term instruments. Whatever their reasons, these investors want a quick turnaround on their money without any risk to their capital. Treasury bills, with their short-term maturities and U.S. Government-backed safety, fulfill this need admirably.

Thus, for the individual investor or the institutional one, Treasury bills offer the convenience of short-term investment with safety and liquidity (convertibility to cash) unduplicated anywhere in the world.

We might say that from the point of view of the U.S. Government, the purpose of a Treasury bill is to make it as easy, convenient, and attractive as possible for an investor to lend money to the United States of America.

Understanding Treasury Bills

Getting Started

Marketability

Treasury bills are *marketable*, which is to say that the bills are negotiable and can be resold at a price that approximates the maturity value. Once they have been issued in the original by the Treasury, they can be bought and sold on what is known as the secondary market. The secondary market negotiation is usually handled through a financial institution, such as a bank, broker, or a dealer in investment securities. It is also possible to buy and sell Treasury bills privately, but this is not common practice.

Bills bought direct from the U.S. Treasury must be transferred to a broker before they can be sold. This transfer cannot be made during the first 20 days after purchase or in the last 20 days before maturity. Whether you buy your Treasury bills direct from the U.S. Treasury or through a financial institution or broker, you can sell them before maturity. But you can sell *only* through a secondary (commercial) market. You cannot sell your Treasury bills back to the U.S. Treasury.

Treasury bills do *not* carry a stated interest rate. Treasury bills are sold at what is called "discount from par." Par is a term meaning 100 cents on the dollar. The purchaser buys the Treasury bill at a percentage *less* than *face value* of the bill. At maturity, the purchaser receives the full, face value of the bill. Since he or she paid less than face value at the time of purchase, the difference between the price paid originally and the face value represents the profit, or *yield*.

It is important to remember that Treasury bills are sold at a discount and redeemed at face value at maturity. Your return is the difference between the purchase price and the face value (if you hold the bill to maturity). This return is termed the *discount* and is based on the par value of the bills.

To sum up, if you buy a Treasury bill you will pay

less than the face value of the bill. If you hold the bill to maturity, the Government will pay you the *full face value*. The difference between what you paid for the bill and its face value is your *yield*. For tax purposes, the IRS considers this yield to be the same as *interest*, such as on a savings account.

Callability

A *callable* security is one that may be redeemed prior to the maturity date by the issuer under certain conditions. Marketable U.S. Treasury securities are not callable, unless specifically labeled. At the time of purchase, investors will be advised if their securities are subject to call.

Get-Started Information Kit

For a complete package of information on Treasury securities, including Treasury bills, write to:
  Bureau of Public Debt
  Division of Customer Services
  300 13th Street, S.W.
  Washington, D.C. 20239-0001
Or, you can telephone 202-287-4113.
Hearing-impaired persons can telephone 202-287-4097.
This information packet is free of charge.

Where Prices Are Listed

Prices of Treasury bills are listed in the financial sections of all major newspapers. Two major financial newspapers also carry quotations on Treasury bills. They are *Barron's*, a weekly, which comes out on Mondays, and *The Wall Street Journal*, a daily. Both can be addressed at 200 Liberty Street, New York, NY 10281. Subscriptions are available by mail, and individual issues are on sale at newsstands.

How To Read Tables

It is important to understand that the prices of Treasury bills are quoted differently than stocks and bonds.

Prices for Treasury bills listed in newspapers are for those bills that the U.S. Treasury has *already issued*. They represent over-the-counter quotations based upon one million dollars or more. The days to maturity are calculated from issue date.

Treasury bill prices are determined by competitive bidding at auctions held by the Treasury. All bills are sold on a discount basis, that is, they are sold at a price below the face value of the bill.

A typical newspaper listing will show the various bill issues in order of maturity dates, from maturity of the shortest term issue to the longest term issue.

Sample Table

The *yield* column listed in the newspaper table shows the true yield equivalent and gives a better picture of what you will earn on your investment.

Treasury Bills

Maturity 1992	Days to Mat.	Bid	Asked	Yield
May 21	6	3.42	3.32	3.38
May 28	13	3.37	3.27	3.33
Jun 04	20	3.57	3.47	3.53
Jun 11	27	3.51	3.41	3.48
Jun 18	34	3.59	3.55	3.62
Jun 25	41	3.52	3.48	3.55
Jul 02	48	3.57	3.53	3.61
Jul 09	55	3.56	3.52	3.60
Jul 16	62	3.57	3.55	3.63
Jul 23	69	3.57	3.55	3.63
Jul 30	76	3.58	3.56	3.45
Aug 06	83	3.59	3.57	3.66
Aug 13	90	3.59	3.57	3.66
Aug 20	97	3.59	3.57	3.66
Aug 27	104	3.61	3.59	3.69

The left-hand column lists all the bills coming due during the period, usually about a year. Therefore, if you are interested in purchasing a Treasury bill with a certain maturity date—say you want to invest your money for a specific time period—you can choose accordingly.

The second column will list the number of days to maturity. If, for example, you have a sum of money that you know you will need in a matter of days, but you don't need it in the meantime, you can choose an issue maturing on a particular date that suits your needs.

The next two columns are headed *Bid* and *Asked* and represent the prices for the previous day as quoted by the professional dealers.

The *Bid* price is the amount that was offered through the auction for that particular issue on that particular day. Remember, all Treasury bills are first sold at auction by the U.S. Treasury before being traded on the secondary market.

The *Asked* price means that the issue is being sold at a price equivalent to a yield of the percentage listed in the *Asked* column.

All Treasury bills are originally issued through the auction process. The auction results provide information regarding the range of accepted discount rates (that is, how much less than face value the bill may be sold for) as well as equivalent prices and investment rates. The discount rate is always based on the par value of the bills. The discount rate is based on a 360-day year (twelve thirty-day months).

The far right-hand column on a Treasury bill table is titled *Yield*. This yield figure will differ from the *Asked* yield because, though Treasury bills are sold on the basis of yield, this does not reflect the "true yield," which is the actual profit derived if the bill is held to maturity.

How to Compute True Yield

For Treasury bills maturing in three or six months, the following formula will give the approximate yield:

Investment Yield =

$$\frac{\text{Face Value minus Purchase Price}}{\text{Purchase Price}} \times \frac{365 \text{ (366 if Leap Year)}}{\text{no. days to maturity}}$$

If, for example, a bill for 182 days (six months) was sold at $9,691.60 per $10,000 face value, to calculate the yield you would proceed as follows:

STEP ONE:

$$\frac{10,000 - 9,691.60}{9,691.60} \quad \text{x} \quad \frac{365}{182}$$

STEP TWO:

$$\frac{308.40}{9,691,60} \quad \text{x} \quad \frac{365}{182}$$

STEP THREE:

$$.0318213 \quad \text{x} \quad 2.0055 = .063818$$

To change the result into a percent, move the decimal two places to the right. The result is 6.3818 percent. This is the "annualized" rate of return. It can be compared to the percentage you might earn if you left your money in a savings account.

Want to Know More About Computing Interest Rates?

For further information on computing returns on Treasury securities, send for the free publication, "The Arithmetic of Interest Rates." It is available from the Public Information Division of the Federal Reserve Bank of New York at 33 Liberty Street, New York, NY 10045.

Individual Investors

Individual investors can purchase Treasury bills directly from the U.S. Treasury or through a bank or broker in initial amounts of $10,000 and in increments of $5,000.

Institutional Investors

Treasury bills are an investment vehicle of choice for many institutional investors, especially mutual funds (see chapter 7). If you are considering shares in some fund, you can ask if they buy Treasuries.

THREE

Treasury Bill Yields

Defining Yields

Put simply, the *yield* on a Treasury bill is the amount of interest you will earn by buying the security, whether you hold it to the full term of maturity or not.

The concept of yield is familiar: we speak of getting a return of 5 percent, or 8 percent, or 10 percent, or 15 percent when we invest our money. We also call the yield the interest rate. For example, we ask what interest the bank is currently paying on savings accounts, or CDs, or checking accounts. Whatever profit we make through the rate of interest is called the *yield*.

In a bank account, your yield may vary with the amount of interest the bank is paying during a particular time period. Time-deposit accounts may have a fixed yield for the period of deposit.

In a money market account or mutual fund, instead of depositing your money you purchase shares in the fund, which then pays you a certain percentage per share as your yield. For all practical purposes, you figure your yield the same way as you do money in the bank.

Treasury bills are quoted on the basis of yield, which means that you pay a specified *price* for the bill which is lower than its face value; then, when you redeem your bill at maturity (or sell it earlier), the difference between what you paid (the price) and what you receive is the yield. This is usually expressed as a percentage (see the table on p. 21).

Remember, a Treasury bill is a *debt security*, which means that the *higher* the price you pay, the *lower* the yield. Conversely, the *lower* the price, the *higher* the yield.

The relationship between yields and maturities can be expressed by a "yield curve," shown in the charts that follow. When the yield curve is *normal*, your profit is greater on longer term maturities. The rule of thumb for the normal yield curve is, "The longer the maturity, the higher the yield."

Normal Yield Curve

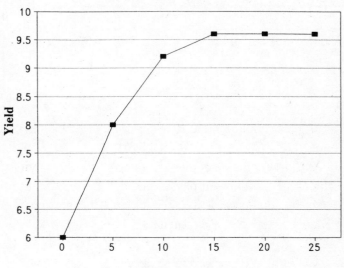

Term to Maturity

However, when returns on short-term securities, such as Treasury bills, are greater than those on the longer term issues (such as notes and bonds), an *inverted yield curve* comes into play and the above rule is reversed to, "The shorter the maturity, the higher the yield."

When an inverted yield curve is in effect, you can buy Treasury bills (short term) and enjoy the rewards of higher yields.

Inverted Yield Curve

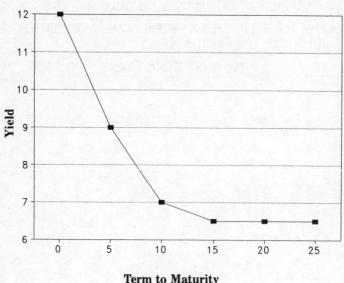

Term to Maturity

History of Yields
on Treasury Bills

Below is a table showing the yields of Treasury bills from 1941 through 1991, for 91-day bills. Yields are listed by the month, January through December.

As you can see, yields in the 1940s were below 1 percent and only began to rise above that in 1949, again dropping below 1 percent in 1954. Thereafter, they continued to increase—with some brief down-turns—to a peak in 1981 of over 16 percent in May of that year. Since 1981, yields on Treasury bills have

91-Day Bill Rate-Avg.
for Last Offering of Month

	Jan.	Feb.	Mar.	Apr.	May	June	July	Aug.	Sept.	Oct.	Nov.	Dec.
1941	NEG.	.086	.055	.097	.107	.087	.094	.090	.062	.151	.242	.310
1942	.220	.222	.221	.335	.365	.360	.372	.367	.373	.373	.368	.357
1943	.369	.369	.374	.373	.374	.375	.374	.375	.375	.375	.375	.373
1944	.374	.375	.375	.374	.375	.375	.375	.375	.375	.375	.375	.373
1945	.375	.375	.376	.375	.375	.375	.375	.375	.375	.375	.375	.373
1946	.375	.375	.375	.376	.376	.376	.376	.375	.375	.376	.376	.374
1947	.376	.376	.376	.376	.376	.376	.740	.766	.817	.895	.944	.952
1948	.990	.997	.996	.997	.997	.998	.997	1.072	1.109	1.120	1.147	1.157
1949	1.160	1.164	1.162	1.156	1.159	1.158	1.017	1.031	1.076	1.036	1.052	1.087
1950	1.103	1.132	1.145	1.166	1.167	1.172	1.174	1.285	1.324	1.316	1.383	1.382
1951	1.389	1.390	1.507	1.506	1.600	1.527	1.591	1.645	1.647	1.593	1.609	1.865
1952	1.589	1.563	1.592	1.616	1.728	1.682	1.877	1.899	1.635	1.757	1.931	2.228
1953	1.961	2.070	2.036	2.243	2.084	1.954	2.157	2.001	1.634	1.220	1.488	1.574
1954	0.998	0.986	1.030	0.886	0.718	0.635	0.800	0.983	0.984	1.007	0.897	1.175
1955	1.349	1.355	1.374	1.697	1.471	1.401	1.720	1.875	2.122	2.231	2.440	2.688
1956	2.245	2.429	2.422	2.788	2.573	2.535	2.303	2.832	2.986	2.907	3.174	3.217
1957	3.283	3.288	3.034	3.054	3.245	3.232	3.158	3.497	3.534	3.622	3.158	3.174
1958	2.202	1.202	1.189	1.055	0.635	1.006	0.984	2.162	2.511	2.647	2.723	2.739
1959	2.975	2.589	2.766	2.831	2.878	3.281	3.047	3.824	3.958	4.022	4.279	4.516
1960	4.116	4.168	2.792	3.317	3.497	2.399	2.404	2.518	2.286	2.129	2.396	2.120
1961	2.230	2.496	2.392	2.186	2.354	2.219	2.244	2.321	2.233	2.325	2.606	2.594
1962	2.688	2.664	2.719	2.740	2.656	2.792	2.892	2.806	2.749	2.742	2.853	2.894
1963	2.917	2.870	2.919	2.884	2.974	2.979	3.206	3.396	3.379	3.452	3.480	3.522
1964	3.501	3.547	3.550	3.446	3.475	3.478	3.475	3.513	3.542	3.567	3.758	3.867

Year												
1965	3.848	3.989	3.922	3.916	3.889	3.789	3.803	3.855	3.983	4.040	4.104	4.457
1966	4.596	4.696	4.555	4.630	4.641	4.435	4.818	5.087	5.503	5.246	5.202	4.747
1967	4.486	4.538	4.150	3.715	3.477	3.462	4.423	4.490	4.629	4.542	4.957	4.989
1968	4.846	5.063	5.186	5.499	5.696	5.238	5.190	5.194	5.182	5.471	5.488	6.199
1969	6.167	6.080	6.065	6.053	6.124	6.456	7.172	7.098	7.106	7.030	7.476	8.096
1970	7.888	6.812	6.330	6.876	7.133	6.421	6.345	6.342	5.807	5.831	5.084	4.803
1971	4.201	3.497	3.521	3.865	4.344	5.080	5.554	4.549	4.676	4.443	4.324	3.731
1972	3.367	3.446	3.849	3.513	3.762	4.023	3.794	4.332	4.644	4.767	4.886	5.111
1973	5.689	5.811	6.251	6.278	6.694	7.228	8.320	8.778	7.331	7.163	7.695	7.406
1974	7.778	7.188	8.300	8.909	7.983	7.841	7.698	9.908	7.002	7.892	7.328	7.113
1975	5.606	5.455	5.562	5.716	5.206	5.665	6.318	6.593	6.547	5.685	5.520	5.208
1976	4.763	4.870	4.929	4.909	5.495	5.368	5.194	5.091	5.072	4.929	4.466	4.296
1977	4.720	4.708	4.609	4.518	4.993	4.965	5.163	5.574	5.982	6.278	6.057	6.144
1978	6.440	6.429	6.310	6.294	6.658	6.967	6.895	7.323	8.106	8.454	9.166	9.388
1979	9.324	9.451	9.498	9.498	9.526	8.802	9.154	9.855	9.989	12.256	11.018	12.105
1980	12.038	13.700	15.037	10.788	7.675	8.149	8.221	10.124	11.524	12.331	14.384	13.908
1981	15.199	14.103	12.501	14.190	16.750	13.909	15.065	15.583	14.669	13.352	10.400	11.690
1982	13.364	12.430	13.399	12.469	11.520	13.269	10.550	8.604	7.801	8.031	8.280	7.975
1983	8.122	7.944	8.680	8.150	8.650	9.090	9.130	9.280	8.730	8.410	8.900	8.940
1984	8.870	9.200	9.760	9.680	9.830	9.770	10.400	10.600	10.270	9.380	8.430	7.840
1985	7.760	8.360	8.410	7.870	7.220	7.060	7.230	7.070	7.070	7.240	7.150	7.040
1986	6.92	6.96	6.35	6.08	6.17	5.99	5.86	5.32	5.20	5.18	5.53	5.68
1987	5.44	5.40	5.72	5.79	5.70	5.82	5.55	6.19	6.59	5.12	5.49	5.73
1988	5.85	5.62	5.69	5.92	6.53	6.59	6.88	7.26	7.23	7.37	8.05	8.22
1989	8.33	8.73	9.10	8.66	8.32	8.07	7.65	7.94	7.72	7.78	7.63	7.77
1990	7.77	7.72	7.85	7.78	7.80	7.78	7.50	7.49	7.32	7.12	7.02	6.78
1991	6.22	6.01	5.86	5.60	5.46	5.58	5.58	5.40	5.18	5.04	4.44	3.91

SOURCE: Moody's Municipal and Government Manual

3-Month Treasury Bills

Yields

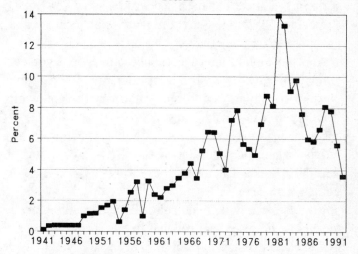

This graph shows a fifty-year history of yields.

fallen steadily and are currently running around 4 percent or less.

However, falling yields on Treasury bills must also be compared to similarly falling rates of interest on CDs and time deposits at banks, and other fixed income investment instruments.

Taxes on Income from Treasury Bills

The bad news is that you must pay federal taxes on all interest you earn on your Treasury bills.

The good news is that earnings on Treasury securi-

23

ties are exempt from state and local taxes. This is particularly good news if you live in a state with a high state income tax. The higher your state tax, the better Treasury bills will look to you! (State and local laws do vary, so check your tax regulations before investing.)

Another advantage to Treasury bills is that you can defer your earnings to the next calendar by the simple method of buying a bill that matures the following year, even if its on January 1.

Since Treasury bill interest equals the difference between the discounted price and the face value at maturity, this is the amount of interest you report on your tax return.

It is possible that if you sell a Treasury bill before it matures, the price you receive might be part interest and part short-term capital gain or loss. If you plan to sell a Treasury bill prior to maturity, you can calculate the interest versus the capital gain by allocating your total discount (the difference between what you paid and the face value of the bill) over the number of days you held the bill prior to its maturity date. If, for example, you bought a bill with a 180-day maturity for $9,500 with a face value of $10,000, you would divide the total discount—in this case $500—by 180 days (the total maturity period) to calculate the amount of interest the bill earns per day: in our example it is $2.77 per day. Then, you multiply that amount by the number of days short of 180 that you actually held the bill. The result will be the amount of interest you have earned. Then, subtract the amount of interest earned from the total you gained by selling the bill. The difference left over is your short-term capital gain.

Should you get *less* gain (due to a fluctuating market) than the amount of prorated interest you would have earned if you held the bill to full term, all of your profit is interest.

An exception to the aforementioned state and local tax exemption on income from Treasury bills is when they are purchased through a mutual fund. In such cases, the tax exemption may or may not apply, depending on the state in which you live. When you purchase through a mutual fund, you buy *shares* in the fund, not the Treasury bills (or securities) themselves. Dividends from a fund may be tax-exempt in some states, but not in all. And different funds may offer different exemptions. Before you purchase through a mutual fund, be sure to check its tax advantages.

Being aware of the tax implications of your investments is important, so don't neglect this aspect. It's a wise idea to consult with your tax advisor before you buy or sell a Treasury bill or other investment. Keeping your tax bill as low as is legally possible, especially over the long haul, is a good part of anyone's investment strategy.

Free Information on the Latest Tax Legislation

For a complimentary copy of the special edition of *U.S. Taxes, Views & Reviews*, an update on changes in the tax law, write to: Tax Update, Price Waterhouse, P.O. Box 30048, Tampa, FL 33630.

Market Risk Factors

U.S. Treasury securities, including Treasury bills, are considered to have no *credit risk*, which is to say that you are guaranteed the full repayment of the money you originally invest. However, like all fixed income securities, Treasury bills are subject to *market risk*.

What market risk means is that if you sell a Treasury bill prior to its maturity date, you could realize a profit or sustain a loss depending on the interest rate trends of the moment. Of course, if you hold the bill to maturity you run no risk whatsoever.

BUYING TREASURY BILLS

Why Buy Treasury Bills?

The primary reason to buy Treasury bills is to acheive a safe and liquid *short-term* investment. While other investment possibilities exist, none are so safe and secure as Treasury securities. Nevertheless, if you are considering buying Treasury bills you should weigh their advantages and disadvantages against alternative investment instruments.

Advantages

• **The Highest Degree of Safety.** The timely payment of interest and principal on U.S. Treasury securities is backed by the full faith and credit of the United States of America. You can be sure of receiving the entire amount of your interest on the precise due date, along with the full return of your principal at maturity.

• **An Uncomplicated Investment.** Treasury bills are easy to understand. In today's increasingly complicated financial market, this can be very reassuring to many people. In addition, Treasuries in general are the benchmark against which other fixed-income securities are valued.

• **Locked-in Interest Rates.** Many investment instruments, such as corporate and municipal bonds, contain "call" provisions, which means that the issuer is allowed to redeem the bond prior to maturity. If bonds are called after interest rates have dropped, which is often the case, investors lose the high rate of interest they had expected to receive for the full term of the security. Furthermore, they are forced to reinvest their money at the prevailing lower rate of interest. As most Treasury securities cannot be called prior to maturity, this risk is avoided when you buy Treasuries. You get an interest rate that is locked in for the full term of your investment.

• **Rate of Return.** When interest rates are rising rapidly, short-term investment instruments such as Treasury bills may yield a better rate of return than long-term bonds. Treasury bills give relatively high yield for short-term investments. (Remember, usually the longer the term, the higher the yield.)

• **Preservation of Capital.** In today's uncertain economic climate, investors want to be sure that their principal investment will be returned at maturity. Treasury bills offer that assurance.

• **Liquidity.** U.S. Treasuries, including Treasury bills, are the most liquid fixed income securities in the world. This is because there is a large, efficient, and well-organized secondary market for them. They are traded constantly, and it is not unusual for the trading volume to surpass $100 billion on a given day.

• **Selection.** Treasury bills come in three-, six-, and twelve-month terms, and a wide range of maturities are available in the highly active commercial market. This makes it easy to find the maturity date that suits your needs.

• **Tax Advantages.** Although taxable at the federal level, U.S. Treasury bills are exempt from state and local income taxes, which can be a big advantage for investors who live in high tax states.

• **Payment of Interest.** Even if you sell them prior to maturity date, Treasury bills pay interest from the date of purchase to the date of sale. There are no penalties for early withdrawal.

• **Commissions.** Treasury bills can be purchased direct from the U.S. Treasury with no commission. Brokered transactions are usually made at a lower commission than on other investment instruments.

• **Banking Alternative.** Treasury bills are an excellent alternative to time-deposit bank accounts.

Disadvantages

• **Capital Required.** Treasury bills require a relatively high amount of capital ($10,000 minimum to start).

• **Inflation Protection.** Treasury bills might not provide a sufficient hedge against inflation. Should interest rate on bills prove to be less than the rate of inflation, you will have a negative real rate of return.

• **Growth Potential.** Treasury bills are low-potential growth investments. Because they are short-term fixed income instruments, they do not give the spectacular results of some higher-risk investments.

Treasury Bills as Part of an Investment Program

Treasury securities can be the foundation of a well-diversified investment portfolio. Every portfolio should rest on a solid base of conservative, high-quality investments, and Treasury securities, including bills, are among the most conservative and highest quality investments available. If one of your goals is to build a balanced portfolio, aimed at protecting you during uncertain economical periods and ensuring prosperity over the long run, Treasury bills merit your most serious consideration.

Whether you are beginning an investment program for the first time or are interested in changing your investment strategy and/or goals, there are three different types of investments that many financial advisors will suggest for your portfolio. The particular mix you choose will depend on the amount of risk you find comfortable:

Cash equivalents. Keeping a portion of your investment dollars in *cash equivalents* lets you maintain liquidity. Money market funds, some of which invest solely in U.S. Treasury securities, let you maintain liquidity by allowing you to write checks against your balance. Treasury bills also offer a high degree of liquidity, but you can sell them only through a broker, usually getting your money on the next business day.

Stocks. Investing in stocks lets you take advantage of changing cycles in the market.

Fixed income investments. Treasury bills and other Treasury securities offer the *stability* of dependable income, even in times of economic insecurity.

Some Investment Terms You Should Know

Accrued Interest — The interest accumulated on a security since the last interest payment. Does not apply to Treasury bills since they do not accrue interest, does apply to Treasury bonds and notes.

Callable — The issuer has the right to redeem or "call" the security prior to the maturity date. Does not usually apply to U.S. Treasury securities, but if it

---

does, you will be informed of the callable condition at the time of purchase.

Current Yield — The amount of annual interest divided by the amount of the initial investment, expressed as a percentage.

Discount Security — A security that is sold at less than face value and matures at full face value. Treasury bills are discount securities.

Face Value — The value appearing on the face of the security, indicating the principal amount the issuer will pay when the security matures and amount on which the interest is calculated. Face value of Treasury bills is always redeemed in full.

Interest — Payments made to compensate the holders of fixed income investments at a fixed percentage during each year the investment is owned. In the case of Treasury bills, the interest is paid *only* at maturity (unless the bill is sold on the secondary market prior to maturity). Interest on Treasury notes and bonds is paid semiannually.

Issuer — The corporation, municipality, or government agency that issues a security. The U.S. Government is the issuer of all Treasury bills, notes, and bonds.

Liquidity — The extent to which an investment can be redeemed or sold quickly for cash without significant loss of value.

Maturity — The date when the principal amount of a fixed income investment is payable by the issuer.

Mutual Fund — A portfolio of diversified securities formed by an investment company, the shares of which are redeemable at their current net asset value. The fund receives professional management and pursues specific investment objectives. Some mutual funds specialize in U.S. Government-only securities (see listing on p. 86).

Par Value — The same as the face value of a security.

Principal — The face amount of a security, payable at maturity.

Secondary Market — The market where previously issued securities are traded. Treasury securities are traded through banks and brokers after the U.S. Treasury has issued and sold them.

Yield to Maturity — The average annual return, taking into account the interest rate, length of time to maturity, and price paid. It is assumed that the security is held until it matures.

Setting Your Investment Goals

Before deciding on the investment mix you want in your portfolio—and how Treasury bills will fit in—it's a wise idea to clarify your investment goals. You need to consider your current income, your capital appreciation, and your taxes.

If, for example, you are waiting for the stock market to improve and are looking for somewhere to "park" your cash in the meantime, Treasury bills could be an attractive bet. Or, you may be looking for some tax advantage. Treasury bills are exempt from state and local taxes. If you are saving for a major purchase in the near future, Treasury bills guarantee the return of your principal with interest on time at the maturity date.

Following the Rules

Once you have defined your goals, you want to ask yourself about risks versus rewards. Because there is less risk of loss with Treasury bills than with some other investment instruments, they generally pay lower yields. The rule historically is: the higher the risk, the higher the reward. Conversely, the lower the risk, the lower the reward.

Another rule to remember is the one that relates the length of time you hold an investment to the return you can expect. Ordinarily, the longer the period of maturity, the higher the yield. Thus, a twelve-month Treasury bill would likely pay a better return than a three-month one. And, of course, holding a bill to maturity will deliver a higher yield.

Interest Rate Fluctuations

Although fluctuating interest rates will not affect a bill held until maturity, be aware that if interest rates fall you do risk getting a lower rate when you reinvest short-term Treasury bills at maturity.

Some investors may want to take advantage of interest rate cycles through Treasury bills. Many analysts suggest that you purchase short-term investments, such as Treasury bills, if you think interest rates will rise. Then, when your Treasury bills reach maturity, if you are correct in your assessment of rising interest rates, you can reinvest at the higher rate rather than being locked in to a lower rate for a longer period of time.

Let's look at some differing examples of life situations and see how Treasury bills might fit into these portfolios:

Suppose you are a young couple just starting out, in your twenties or thirties. Chances are you have a major financial goal in mind—the purchase of a house or capital to start a business. If you are a two-income family, without substantial financial obligations to consider, you may be able to put aside a considerable part of your income to help you reach your goals. Some of that income may be invested in long-term growth instruments, such as stocks and bonds. It may be a wise idea to balance out your portfolio with the safety and liquidity of Treasury bills.

On the other hand, what if you have been married a few years, have young children to care for, and are concerned with planning for their future as well as yours. With the costs of a college education mounting steadily, parents may wonder how they are going to accumulate the needed funds. Such investors may want a high degree of safety for their money and will choose their investments accordingly. For them, a secure foundation for their portfolio would include Treasury bills.

Mature couples with grown children will have different requirements. As they begin to reach their middle years, they will consider all their assets and look at their goals for the coming retirement years. They may be in a high tax bracket and the tax ramifications of their investments may be something to think about seriously. Treasury bills, exempt from state and local taxes, may be an intelligent choice for inclusion in such a portfolio.

When retirement arrives, other than health, nothing is so important to most people as financial independence. Whatever your retirement goals—travel, moving to a warmer climate, pursuing hobbies, spending time with grandchildren—you want the peace of mind that financial security brings. Widows in particular want to be free of money worries. As more people today are retiring earlier than in the years before, they have many active years to look forward to. Fixed income securities provide *guaranteed* income and, because they are a hedge against inflation, Treasury bills might become a substantial part of the base of a retirement investment pyramid.

When to Buy Treasury Bills

It is important to remember that one of the primary advantages of Treasury bills is their *short term*. Therefore, Treasury bills are good investments when you have cash to spare for a short period of time. Of course, you can always reinvest your money in Treasury bills once the maturity date arrives.

Another good opportunity to buy Treasury bills is when you (or your financial advisor) expect interest rates to rise. In such times, limiting market risk by buying Treasury bills with short maturities is a proven defense strategy. The shortening of maturities helps insulate your portfolio from the negative impact of rising interest rates and minimizes your exposure to capital losses.

Professional investors regularly use Treasury bills for short-term investment when their cash flow does not permit a longer term instrument to be viable for their particular needs. They buy Treasury bills because they know they can trust the outcome while getting a reasonable rate of return on their money.

Another time to buy Treasury bills is when you have extra funds that you might otherwise consider putting into a time-deposit account at a bank. Treasury bills are an attractive alternative to the average bank depositor because it is possible for a bank to fail (as witness the Savings and Loan banks collapse). Although the chances of a bank failure are slim, and deposits are protected up to $100,000 per account by the FDIC, in terms of overall safety Treasury bills are more secure.

Auction Schedule

Auctions of three- and six-month bills are usually held every Monday (or the following Tuesday if the Monday is a bank holiday). Auctions of twelve-month bills are usually held every fourth week, on a Thursday. (See chapter 5, "Buying Treasury Bills from the Federal

Reserve Bank," for further information about how to participate in auctions for Treasury bills.)

Two-year and five-year notes are issued at the end of each month.

Seven-year notes are issued every three months in January, April, July, and October.

Three-year to ten-year notes are issued on the 15th of February, May, August, and November of each year.

Ten-year to thirty-year bonds are issued on the 15th of February, May, August, and November.

Minimum Investments

Since the minimum investment for a Treasury bill is $10,000 to start, for some investors, the minimum investment may pose a problem. If that is the case, you can consider investing in a money market or mutual fund that buys only Treasury securities. Many of these firms have lower minimums, typically around $1,000. Institutional investor purchases are in the billions of dollars.

When to Sell Treasury Bills

The obvious answer is to sell when you need to convert your Treasury bill into cash, for whatever reason. Unless there is a sharp rise in interest rates, there is no particularly good or bad time to sell a Treasury bill except that the closer it is to the maturity date the more interest will be earned. The market for Treasury bills is highly liquid, enabling the sale to be made easily.

You can buy Treasury bills and hold them just as long as you wish, from a few days to a year. You can sell whenever you wish, for any reason that suits you. Whenever you sell, you will receive interest for the time you have held the bill.

Rollovers

What about reinvesting your money in Treasury bills as a longer-term proposition? This is done all the time. Many investors simply "roll over" their money, keeping a good part of their capital invested in Treasury bills and continuing to earn interest while retaining the benefits of safety and liquidity. When rolling over your Treasury bill for another term you forfeit none of the advantages of your original purchase. You can even arrange with your Federal Reserve Bank to have your Treasury bills automatically renewed each time they reach maturity.

F I V E

Buying Treasury Bills from the Federal Reserve Bank

Treasury bills, and other Treasury securities, may be purchased direct from the U.S. Treasury. Although many investors buy through banks and brokers (see chapter 6, "Using a Broker") when you buy direct from the Treasury you pay no commissions. The Treasury regularly holds *auctions* to sell its new issues of Treasury bills.

Since August 1, 1986, securities bought through the Treasury Direct system will be maintained for you in "book-entry" form. This means that your account will be kept in computerized form *only* because the Treasury no longer issues engraved certificates. Instead of actual certificates, you will receive a statement of account which will provide you with a record of your Treasury holdings.

Special Note

Up until 1986, the Treasury issued engraved certificates to the buyers of Treasury securities. Today that is no longer the case. Since August 1, 1986, all Treasury securities purchased direct from the Treasury are kept on a computerized "book-entry" system. Although it is no longer possible to purchase either bearer or definitive (registered, engraved certificates) securities from the U.S. Treasury, some of these do still exist and can be purchased on the secondary (commercial) market through financial institutions, brokers, and dealers in investment securities.

This system is both safe and convenient and it provides a number of additional features:

• **Single Master Account.** A special feature of the Treasury Direct book-entry Securities System is the Single Master Account, which contains ownership and payment information about all your marketable Treasury securities having the same registration. Although you may have several Treasury holdings in your portfolio, the details, such as the name(s) in the registration, address, telephone number, and the tax identification number, are maintained within your one account. Thus, record keeping is simplified and tax information is recorded in one place. The system offers built-in flexibility since changes to the details of your account information, such as a change of address, can be made quickly. You will be given a unique account number, much like a bank account number.

• **Account Review.** Your statement of account provides you with a complete record of your entire Treasury securities holdings and other information about your account. You are sent a statement of account whenever a new account is established or information changes on the details of your account, such as where payments are to be made, additional purchases are added, or changes are made to reinvestment status.

• **Direct Access.** Your Treasury Direct account gives you access to your single master account at any Federal Reserve Bank, its branches, or the Treasury—regardless where your account was established. You can make additional transactions, such as purchasing additional Treasury bills (or other Treasury securities), transferring securities from one account to another, or requesting detailed information on the changes to your account at any of 37 locations throughout the United States.

• **Direct Deposit.** When you invest through the Treasury Direct system, you are offered a safe and convenient method of receiving payments from your Treasury investments. Redemption payments are deposited directly into an account at a financial institution of your choice, and you need never worry about lost or stolen checks.

The Treasury will notify the financial institution that it will be receiving electronic payments of funds to be deposited into an account you have designated.

• **Reinvestment Option.** With its *multiple automatic reinvestment option*, the Treasury Direct book-entry system offers you more versatility than ever before when you invest in Treasury bills securities. With Treasury Direct, you can request multiple, automatic reinvestments of your 13-, 26- or 52-week Treasury bills. You can schedule these reinvestments for up to two years after the first maturity date without having to complete and mail a reinvestment request each time you want to reinvest your bill.

• **Registration Options.** When you purchase from Treasury Direct, you have available a broad choice of registration options designed to address most investor needs and ownership situations, which provide the ability to establish clear ownership and survivorship rights to securities.

Registration Options

Single ownership—Resistration is in the name of an individual. The name should be in the form ordinarily used by the investor, preferably including at least one full given name.

Joint ownership with Right of Survivorship—Registration is in the names of two individuals, joined by the word *and*, ending with "right of survivorship." Transaction requests must be signed by both owners. This form of registration creates a conclusive right of survivorship.

Joint ownership without Right of Survivorship—Registration is in the names of two individuals, joined by the word *and*, ending with "without right of survivorship." Transactions requests must be signed by both owners. This form of ownership does not create a right of survivorship. The share of the decedent passes to his or her estates.

Co-ownership—Registration is in the names of two individuals, joined by the word *or*. Transaction requests may be signed by either co-owner. This form of registration creates a conclusive right of survivorship.

Beneficiary—Registration is in the name of one individual, followed by the words *payable on death to* (P.O.D.) another individual. If a minor or an incompetent is named as beneficiary, the beneficiary's status must be identified in the registration. Transaction requests may be signed by the owner and do not require the consent of the beneficiary. Ownership rights are transferred to the beneficiary only after the death of the owner.

Natural Guardian—Registration is in the name of a natural guardian of a minor (a security may not be registered in the name of a minor in his or her own right). Transaction requests are signed by the natural guardian (parents) on behalf of the minor until the qualification of a legal guardian or similar representative, or the minor's attainment of majority.

Custodian—Registration is under an applicable gifts to minors statute. Any request to alter the ownership rights must be made as provided in the applicable statute.

Estate Representative—Registration is in the name of the executor, administrator, legal guardian, conservator, or similar representative of an estate. The name of the estate must be adequately identified in the registration. If there is more than one representative, some names may be omitted in language that indicates their existence. Those named in the registration will be presumed to have the authority to sign transaction requests on behalf of all of the representatives.

Trustees—Registration is in the name(s) of the trustee(s) of a trust, followed by adequate identification of the authority by which the trust was created. If there is more than one trustee, some names may be omitted in language that indicates their existence. Those named in the registration will be presumed to have the authority to sign transaction requests on behalf of all of the trustees.

Private Organizations—Registration is in the name of a private corporation, unincorporated association, or partnership. The full legal name and status (corporation, unincorporated association, or partnership) must be included in the registration. The registration may reference a particular account or fund (other than a trust fund).

Governmental Entities and Officers—Registration is in the name of a state, county, city, town, village, school district, or other governmental entity. If a governmental officer is authorized to act as trustee or custodian, registration may be in the title (or name and title) of the officer. The registration must reflect the capacity in which the officer is authorized to hold property.

SOURCE: PD 5210, U.S. Government Printing Office, Department of the Treasury, Bureau of Public Debt

Disadvantages of Purchasing Treasury Bills Direct

Although there are many attractive advantages to purchasing Treasury bills through the Treasury Direct system, some disadvantages must also be considered:

• **Availability of Cash.** Although your Treasury bill is negotiable, and as such considered liquid, in order to sell a Treasury bill bought direct from the Treasury *prior to maturity* you must employ a broker to handle the transaction. You must fill out a form authorizing the Treasury to transfer your account to the broker or financial institution (bank) you have designated to sell your security. Prior to the transaction, you must make arrangements with the institution that is to receive the transfer. A request for transfer must be received not later than 20 days before maturity.

• **Previously Issued Treasury Bills.** Only new issues of Treasury bills can be bought from the Treasury Direct. If you wish to buy previously issued Treasury bills, you must act through a bank or a broker.

• **Timing.** Treasury bills can only be bought from Treasury Direct at scheduled auctions. Should you want to make a purchase at a time when an auction is not being held, you must use a bank or a broker as your agent.

Treasury Direct

For complete information and the regulations for purchasing Treasury bills from the government, that is, Treasury Direct, see Department of the Treasury Circular, Public Debt Series No. 2–86(31 CFR Part 357).

Federal Reserve Bank Addresses

Following is a list of all the Federal Reserve banks in the United States. These are also known as *servicing offices* for Treasury Direct. The U.S. Government makes it easy for you to buy its Treasury securities and to receive information about them. No matter where you live you can call or visit the servicing office nearest you to make transactions on your account or to receive information about your Treasury securities investments or about new issues of Treasury securities.

For convenience sake, addresses are listed both for in-person visits and for written correspondence. Please note the difference. If you want to *visit* a servicing office, use the street address shown in the left-hand column. Visiting hours may vary from bank to bank, so it is always wise to telephone in advance and check the bank's opening and closing times. To *write* to a servicing office, use the addresses shown in the right-hand column.

For In-Person Visits:	For Written Correspondence:
104 Marietta Street, N.W. Atlanta, Georgia **404-521-8657** (Recording) **404-521-8653**	104 Marietta Street, N.W. Atlanta, GA 30303
502 South Sharp Street Baltimore, Maryland **301-576-3300**	P.O. Box 1378 Baltimore, MD 21203
FRB Birmingham 1801 Fifth Avenue, North Birmingham, Alabama **205-252-3141 Ext. 215** (Recording) **205-252-3141 Ext. 264**	P.O. Box 10447 Birmingham, AL 35283

For In-Person Visits:	For Written Correspondence:
FRB Boston 600 Atlantic Avenue Boston, Massachusetts **617-973-3805** (Recording) **617-973-3810**	P.O. Box 2076 Boston, MA 02106
FRB Buffalo 160 Delaware Avenue **716-849-5046** (Recording) **716-849-5030**	P.O. Box 961 Buffalo, NY 14240-0961
FRB Charlotte 401 South Tryon Street Charlotte, North Carolina **704-336-7100**	P.O. Box 30248 Charlotte, NC 28230
FRB Chicago 230 South La Salle Street Chicago, Illinois **312-786-1110** (Recording) **312-322-5369**	P.O. Box 834 Chicago, IL 60690
FRB Cincinnati 150 East Fourth Street Cincinnati, Ohio **513-721-4787 Ext. 334**	P.O. Box 999 Cincinnati, OH 45201
FRB Cleveland 1455 East Sixth Street Cleveland, Ohio **216-579-2490**	P.O. Box 6387 Cleveland, OH 44101
FRB Dallas 400 South Akard Street Dallas, Texas **214-651-6362**	Securities Dept. Station K 400 South Akard Street Dallas, TX 75222

Buying Treasury Bills from the Federal Reserve Bank

For In-Person Visits:	For Written Correspondence:
FRB Denver 1020 16th Street Denver, Colorado 303-572-2475 (Recording) 303-572-2470 or 2473	P.O. Box 5228 Terminal Annex Denver, CO 80217
FRB Detroit 160 West Fort Street Detroit, Michigan 313-964-6153 (Recording) 313-964-6157	P.O. Box 1059 Detroit, MI 48231
FRB Houston 1701 San Jacinto Street Houston, Texas 713-659-4433	P.O. Box 2578 Houston, TX 77001
FRB Jacksonville 800 West Water Street Jacksonville, Florida 904-632-1179	P.O. Box 2499 Jacksonville, FL 32231-2499
FRB Kansas City 925 Grand Avenue Kansas City, Missouri 816-881-2767 (Recording) 816-881-2409	P.O. Box 440 Kansas City, MO 64198
FRB Little Rock 325 West Capitol Avenue Little Rock, Arkansas 501-372-5451 Ext. 273	P.O. Box 1261 Little Rock, AR 72203
FRB Los Angeles 950 South Grand Avenue Los Angeles, California 213-624-7398	P.O. Box 2077 Terminal Avenue Los Angeles, CA 90051

For In-Person Visits:	For Written Correspondence:
FRB Louisville 410 South Fifth Street Louisville, Kentucky 502-568-9232 (Recording) 502-568-9236 or 9238	P.O. Box 32710 Louisville, KY 40232
FRB Memphis 200 North Main Street Memphis, Tennessee 901-523-7171 Ext. 225 or 641	P.O. Box 407 Memphis, TN 38101
FRB Miami 9100 N.W. Thirty-Sixth Street Miami, Florida 305-593-9923 (Recording) 305-591-2065	P.O. Box 520847 Miami, FL 33152
FRB Minneapolis 250 Marquette Avenue Minneapolis, Minnesota 612-340-2075	250 Marquette Avenue Minneapolis, MN 55480
FRB Nashville 301 Eighth Avenue, North Nashville, Tennessee 615-259-4006	301 Eighth Avenue, North Nashville, TN 37203
FRB New Orleans 525 St. Charles Avenue New Orleans, Louisiana 504-522-1659 (Recording) 504-586-1505 Ext. 293	P.O. Box 61630 New Orleans, LA 70161

For In-Person Visits:	For Written Correspondence:
FRB New York 33 Liberty Street New York, New York 212-720-5823 (Recording) 212-720-6619	Federal Reserve P.O. Station New York, NY 10045
FRB Oklahoma City 226 Dean A. McGee Avenue Oklahoma City, Oklahoma 405-270-8660 (Recording) 405-270-8652	P.O. Box 25129 Oklahoma City, OK 73125
FRB Omaha 2201 Farnam Street Omaha, Nebraska 402-221-5638 (Recording) 402-221-5633	2201 Farnam Street Omaha, NE 68102
FRB Philadelphia Ten Independence Mall Philadelphia, Pennsylvania 215-574-6580 (Recording) 215-574-6680	P.O. Box 90 Philadelphia, PA 19105
FRB Pittsburgh 717 Grant Street Pittsburgh, Pennsylvania 412-261-7988 (Recording) 412-261-7863	P.O. Box 867 Pittsburgh, PA 15230-0867
FRB Portland 915 S.W. Stark Street Portland, Oregon 503-221-5931 (Recording) 503-221-5932	P.O. Box 3436 Portland, OR 97208

For In-Person Visits:	For Written Correspondence:
FRB Richmond 701 East Byrd Street Richmond, Virginia **804-697-8000**	P.O. Box 27622 Richmond, VA 23261
FRB Salt Lake City 120 South State Street Salt Lake City, Utah **801-322-7911** (Recording) **801-355-3131**	P.O. Box 30780 Salt Lake City, UT 84130
FRB San Antonio 126 East Nueva Street San Antonio, Texas **512-224-2141 Ext. 311** (Recording) **512-224-2141 Ext. 303** or **305**	P.O. Box 1471 San Antonio, TX 78295
FRB San Francisco 101 Market Street San Francisco, California **415-882-9798** (Recording) **415-974-2330**	P.O. Box 7702 San Francisco, CA 94120
FRB Seattle 1015 Second Avenue Seattle, Washington **206-442-1650** (Recording) **206-442-1652**	Securities Services Dept. P.O. Box 3567 Terminal Annex Seattle, WA 98124
FRB St. Louis 411 Locust Street St. Louis, Missouri **314-444-8602** (Recording) **314-444-8665**	P.O. Box 14915 St. Louis, Mo 63178

For In-Person Visits:	For Written Correspondence:
United States Treasury Washington, DC	
	Mail **Inquiries** to:
Bureau of the Public Debt Securities Transactions Branch 1300 C Street, S.W. Washington, DC 202-287-4113	Bureau of the Public Debt Division of Customer Services 300 13th Street, S.W. Washington, DC 20239-0001
Device for hearing impaired 202-287-4097	Mail **Tenders** to: Bureau of the Public Dept Department N Washington, DC 20239-1500

Some Important Definitions

Bill—A short-term obligation of the U.S. Treasury with a maturity of 13, 26, or 52 weeks.

Auction—A sale that determines the price and interest (yield) of Treasury securities. The public is not allowed to witness bid openings.

Bidders—There are two categories of bids for Treasury securities:

1. *Competitive*: usually submitted by financial institutions or securities dealers/brokers.
2. *Noncompetitive*: usually submitted by individuals and others who receive the average price and interest rate of the accepted competitive bids.

Book-Entry—Computerized record of ownership of Treasury securities.

Statement of Account—A record mailed to the owner noting newly purchased and other previously purchased securities held in his or her account.

Discount on Bills—The security is considered to be sold at a discount if the auction price of the security is lower than the face value.

Reinvestment/Rollover—Treasury bills may automatically be reinvested (called a *rollover*), upon request, at maturity.

Registration—The form of ownership in which the account (or accounts) is held.

Federal Reserve Bank Auctions

Offering Schedule for Bills

Three series of Treasury bills are offered on a regular basis. Two series of bills, one having a 13-week and the other a 26-week term, are offered each week. The pattern of weekly bill issues is as follows (except when holidays or special situations occur):

1. The offering is announced on Tuesday.
2. The bills are auctioned the following Monday.
3. The bills are issued on the Thursday following the auction.

Bills with a 52-week term are usually offered every four weeks as follows:

1. The offering is announced on a Friday.
2. The bills are auctioned the following Thursday.
3. The bills are issued on the Thursday following the auction.

Bill Sales Procedures

As we have said earlier, the minimum bid for a Treasury bill is $10,000 and in multiples of $5,000 over that. Tenders (applications) may be submitted *competitively* or *noncompetitively*.

Most competitive bids are made by institutional investors, such as commercial banks and brokers who purchase large amounts of securities. These bids specify the amount of yield the bidder is willing to accept (expressed in a percentage, such as *6.25%*). When making a competitive bid, there is the risk of bidding too high and not getting an allotment of the security, since the Treasury usually accepts only the lowest bids. Therefore, depending on the overall results, orders will be filled or rejected.

In the auction process, competitive tenders are accepted beginning with those bidding for the lowest discount rate (percentage of yield), through successively higher rates, to the extent required to attain the amount that the Treasury had planned to borrow on that day. *All noncompetitive tenders are accepted.*

Under competitive bidding, if the investor's bid does not fall in the range of accepted bids, that investor risks paying more than the noncompetitive price, or not being able to acquire the security at all.

Therefore, *most individual investors submit non-*

competitive tenders (bids), which do not require that a yield be specified. These individuals agree to accept the average yield and equivalent price determined by the accepted competitive tenders. Noncompetitive bidders do not risk rejection of their bid.

There is no limit on the amount you may purchase in any one name by competitive tender. However, noncompetitive tenders in any one name are limited to one million dollars for each new offering.

Auction results are announced by the Treasury in the late afternoon of the auction day. This information can be found in the financial section of most newspapers the following day.

Where Auctions are Listed

Auction information can be found in the financial sections of most newspapers. Some Federal Reserve banks maintain 24-hour recorded message services to announce the exact date and times of Treasury offerings and results of auctions. Ask your local Federal Reserve Bank to give you this number.

How To Participate in an Auction

You may buy Treasury bills in person or by mail by submitting a bid, or tender. Your order can be submitted on an official tender form (available from your Federal Reserve Bank). You may use the following forms to purchase a Treasury bill:

- Tender for 13-week Treasury Bill (PD 5176–1)
- Tender for 26-week Treasury Bill (PD 5176–2)
- Tender for 52-week Treasury Bill (PD 5176–3)

The Department of the Treasury will establish and maintain the book-entry account for securities purchased using any of these forms.

You may also tender by letter.

Tenders must be received by 12 P.M. on the date of the auction if submitted in person. If by mail, bids must be postmarked by midnight of the day preceding the auction date *and* must be received on or before the issue date of the bill.

How To Submit a Bid

If submitting with a Treasury form, fill out the form as indicated. If submitting your bid by letter, provide the following information:

Tender Information

Amount of tender—Give the total amount of the bill you are offering to buy. The amount must be at least $10,000 and a multiple of $5,000. The total amount of noncompetitive tenders from a single bidder may not exceed $1,000,000 for the same offering of securities.
Bid Type—Specify noncompetitive.
Account number—If the securities are to be added to an existing Treasury Direct account, give the Account Number. If no Account Number exists, the Treasury will open an account for you.

To establish *direct deposit* for your investment payments, furnish the following information:

1. The name of the financial institution in which you want your payments deposited.
2. The name(s) of the account designated to receive direct deposit payments.
3. The account number to which the direct deposit payments should be made.
4. Nine-digit American Bankers Association Routing Transit Number of the designated financial institution (this can be found at the bottom of a check or deposit slip or by contacting the financial institution).

Payments to you will normally be made by direct deposit to the financial institution you specify. If both the Treasury Direct account and the receiving financial institution account are in the names of individuals, then at least one of the individuals named on the Treasury Direct account must also be named on the deposit account at the receiving financial institution.

Investor Information

Account Name—Enter the name(s) of the owner(s) for whom the Treasury Direct account will be established. If the tender is for an existing account, enter the name from the Statement of Account. Accounts may be established in the names of one or two individuals, an estate, a trust, corporation, association, etc.

Address—Provide a complete address, including zip

code. All mailings, including notices, statements, and checks, will be sent to this address.

Telephone Numbers—Provide the telephone numbers (including area codes) where you may be contacted if there are questions about the tender or your account.

Taxpayer Identification Number

Provide the taxpayer identification number required on tax returns and other documents submitted to the Internal Revenue Service. For individuals, this is the social security number (SSN) of the person whose name appears *first* on the account. The SSN of a minor or incompetent is required for accounts established in a fiduciary capacity for these individuals. In the case of a partnership, company, organization, or trust, the employer identification number assigned by the IRS is used.

Signature

The tender must be signed with your legal signature.

How To Pay

Full payment for the *face value* of the tender offer must be submitted with your bid. Payment may be made in any of the following ways:

1. **Checks** issued by banks, savings and loan associations, or credit unions. Personal checks (these must be certified).

Checks must be payable to the institution to which they are submitted (that is, to the Federal Reserve Bank or branch, or to the Bureau of the Public Debt). Checks submitted to the Bureau of the Public Debt that are made payable to a Federal Reserve Bank or Branch are not acceptable, and any such check sent to Public Debt will cause the tender to be rejected. No two-party checks will be accepted.

2. **Cash** must be presented in person.
3. **Treasury Securities**. Payment may be made with Treasury securities maturing on or before the issue date.

Negotiability of Treasury Bills

In past years, the Treasury issued both *bearer* and *registered* definitive securities, many of which have not reached maturity. These were issued as engraved certificates. Although they are no longer sold by the Treasury in original issues, these earlier issues can be purchased on the secondary market (at prevailing market prices) through financial institutions, brokers, and dealers in investment securities.

A *bearer security* is a highly negotiable security, payable to anyone who has possession of the certificate. No owner's name is shown. Like a check made out to *Cash*, a bearer security is in effect cash and, for that reason, the security should be safeguarded as carefully as cash.

A *registered security* has the owner's name and

taxpayer identification number printed on the front of the security. Ownership is recorded on the books of the Treasury. Registered securities may not be sold or have ownership transferred without the written assignment of the registered owner. An assignment form is printed on the back of the security.

Treasury securities represented by engraved certificates may be redeemed at maturity for face value at any Federal Reserve Bank or branch or at the Bureau of the Public Debt in Washington, D.C. To redeem by mail, registered mail should be used.

Reinvesting

When you invest in Treasury bills via the Treasury Direct system, you may request reinvestment or multiple automatic reinvestments of 13-, 26-, or 52-week bills for up to two years after the first maturity date without having to complete an additional reinvestment request each time the bill comes to maturity.

For example, should you have a Treasury Direct account in which you are holding a bill, prior to maturity of the security you will receive by mail a notice advising you that the security is about to mature. The notice will list the options available to you. In general, bill holders will be eligible to reinvest in bills of various terms.

If the maturing security is a Treasury bill, the notice will be in computerized form and you have only to fill it in, sign it, date it, and forward it to the address provided.

Here are some questions commonly asked about reinvesting through the Treasury Direct system:

Q. *Can I reinvest only part of the proceeds from my maturing Treasury bills?*

A. Yes. Provided you reinvest an authorized amount and you make your request through your local FRB servicing office. Your servicing office will provide you with the proper form for reinvesting a partial amount. The machine readable form you receive by mail cannot be used to make a partial reinvestment.

Q. *How soon must I return my request for reinvestment?*

A. Your request to reinvest your maturing security must be received at least 20 calendar days prior to the maturity of the security. The notice you receive will list the date by which you must return the form. If, however, a mail delay occurs and you do not have time to return the form by the required date, simply telephone your local servicing office for assistance.

Q. *How will I know my request for reinvestment was received?*

A. Your Statement of Account will show the change and you can verify that the reinvestment was made correctly.

Multiple Automatic Reinvestment

Q. *How does the Treasury Bill multiple reinvestment option work?*

A. The number of reinvestments available depends

upon the term of the Treasury bill you purchase. The maximum length of reinvestment is two years, or 104 weeks. Thus, for example, a 13-week bill, reinvested each time it matures over a 2-year period, would be scheduled for reinvestment eight times. Similarly, the maximum number of automatic reinvestments for a 26-week bill is four and for a 52-week bill it is two.

Q. *What is the advantage of scheduling multiple automatic reinvestments of my Treasury bills over single-time reinvestment?*

A. Convenience. By scheduling your multiple automatic reinvestments in advance, you no longer need to worry about keeping track of maturity dates or complete a new reinvestment form for each new issue.

Q. *Can I schedule multiple automatic reinvestments for my Treasury bills for less than two years?*

A. Yes. You can schedule reinvestment for shorter periods of time. For a 13-week bill, you can choose two to seven automatic reinvestments; for a 26-week bill, one to three. Or, you can request your reinvestments one at a time.

Q. *May I change my mind after I've chosen my reinvestment schedule?*

A. Yes. You can cancel your previous reinvestment request and change the number of reinvestments for bills if your request is received at least 20 calendar days prior to the maturity of your bill. To do so, ask your servicing office for Form PD 5180, "Reinvestment Request."

Q. *What if I have not scheduled a reinvestment and my security matures?*

A. Your maturing security will be redeemed on the maturity date. Payment will be made according to the payment instructions you previously specified when buying through Treasury Direct.

Where To Get Information on Reinvestment Options

Your local servicing office has all of your account information available under your single master account. Customer service personnel can tell you what reinvestment options are available for your Treasury bills. See the listing of Treasury Direct servicing offices on p. 49.

Special Note

The availability of new Treasury offerings can be altered by Treasury borrowing requirements, financing policy decisions, or the timing of Congressional action on the debt limit. If the maturity date of your security does not coincide, but is within five calendar days of the issue date of the reinvestment option you have selected, the funds will be placed in a non-interest-bearing account until the issue date. If the period is greater than five calendar days, your request for reinvestment will not be processed and your funds will be returned.

Using a Broker

Where Treasury bills are concerned the question is whether to use a broker or not to use a broker. As you have already learned, you can buy your Treasury bills direct from the U.S. Treasury through its Treasury Direct system. This is not the case with regular stocks and bonds for which you *must* use a broker (although there are some exceptions to this rule).

So, having the choice of using a broker to buy your

Treasury bills for you or not using one, what is the best course of action?

Again, this decision rests in part on your own particular needs and your individual aims.

What exactly is a broker? A broker, or a brokerage firm, is an intermediary that you hire to buy and sell your securities for you. It's as simple as that. And you pay a fee for the service.

There are two kinds of brokers: full-service and discount.

The Full-Service Broker

The full-service broker offers a variety of services, including financial advice. As several hundred issues of Treasury securities are outstanding at any one time, and as much as $100 billion in Treasuries are traded on an average day, you may feel you need professional guidance to choose the Treasury bills that are suited to your particular needs. A full-service broker is in a position to serve you with such guidance.

Your full-service broker can assist you in determining appropriate times to invest and can help you to choose the maturities most appropriate to your individual financial goals. He can explain the market environment to you if you are not sure of the situation.

Such a broker's firm will maintain a research department whose analyses are available to you. As your financial consultant, the full-service broker is in a position to keep you apprised of the firm's analysts' opinions and provide you with timely advice so that you can profit from or protect against interest rate fluctuations.

This does not necessarily mean that the person on the telephone has all the answers; you may have to ask for the information you need. However, once you have established a working relationship with a broker, you can indicate that you want to receive market advice on a regular basis.

In addition, you can advise a full-service broker of your investment needs and objectives. Through personal contact and regular transactions, you have the opportunity to develop a relationship with your broker so he can better service your needs and objectives.

The Discount Broker

The discount broker is just that: he operates his business at a discount. So don't expect the same services available through the full-service broker. Naturally, the commissions paid to a discount broker are far less than those paid to the full-service broker. You pay less, you get less. That's the trade-off.

In the case of Treasury bills (and other Treasury securities), commissions are already low so there may not be any advantage to using a discount broker. The rule of thumb is to use a discount broker when you are actively involved in handling your own account as an informed investor.

Let's take a look at situations when a broker is a necessity and the pros and cons of using a broker when you have a choice.

Why Use a Broker?

1. You *must* use a broker if you wish to buy Treasury bills at a time that does not coincide with a public auction.
2. You *must* use a broker if you decide to sell your Treasury bills prior to the date of maturity.
3. You *must* use a broker if you wish your order to be executed immediately. Tendering for an auction takes time.

What Are the Advantages of Using a Broker?

- Transactions are handled swiftly. A broker can buy or sell on the same day the order is given and the transaction can be completed the next day of business. This can give you an edge if you need to sell before maturity, because there will be no delay in executing your sale. On the other hand, if you hold Treasury bills in an account at the Federal Reserve and want to sell, you first must transfer the securities to your brokerage account. Not only is that an inconvenience, it might cost you money—if prices drop before the transfer is completed.
- A broker provides investment flexibility. If you use a broker, you don't have to wait for scheduled Treasury auctions, perhaps running the risk of

interest rates being lower on the actual auction date than an earlier date.

- If you use a broker (as opposed to buying direct from the U.S. Treasury), you can stagger the maturities of your Treasury bills through issues available on the open market. For example, if you spend your winters in Arizona and want maturities to coincide with the time you leave and return, you can purchase Treasury bills that mature in those months.
- A full-service broker can serve as a counselor and provide sound investment advice.
- Some brokerage firms maintain 24-hour 7-day-a-week service lines. With such a broker you can buy or sell your Treasury bills just by picking up the telephone at any hour of the day or night.
- A broker provides a secure place to keep your Treasury bills.
- Brokers simplify your record keeping for you. You get a monthly statement of all your transactions.
- Your investments through a broker are protected by insurance.

What Are the Disadvantages of Using a Broker?

Nothing is perfect. There are *some* disadvantages to using a broker that you might want to consider, especially in the case of Treasury bills.

- **Fees.** Although brokerage fees for handling Treasury bills are usually quite low, you may encounter "hidden" charges and additional fees for some services.
- **Advice.** It is always possible to get bad advice from your broker. The better you know your broker and the better you are known is the best insurance against bad advice. The discount broker does not give investment recommendations. With a discount broker, you are on your own. He merely executes your buy and sell orders.
- **Failure.** Although very few brokerage firms fail, it is a possibility, and one of which you should be aware. However, for most people this is not a major concern. And in any case the broker should be protected by insurance and the large investor can often purchase excess protection. Be sure to ask your broker about his insurance coverage.

How To Find a Broker

What is the best way to find a broker if you don't already have one?

By *referral*.

Ask your family, friends, and co-workers about their experiences with their brokers. If you know someone with a large investment portfolio, or someone professionally involved in the financial business, ask that person.

What if you don't know anyone personally who can provide a referral?

The next-best place to go is your local bank. The chances are you already have a relationship with someone at your bank. It might be the bank manager or a loan officer. If you don't have such a relationship, just speak to one of the bank's officers who sits out front and handles the daily business. Many banks today offer brokerage services, and it may be that your bank can provide for your needs. In any case, the bank's personnel are likely to be well-informed about choosing brokers.

Another source of information is your insurance company. Again, you might already have a relationship with your insurance agent and can ask about choosing a broker. Some insurance companies also offer brokerage services.

Last but not least you can consult the Yellow Pages of your telephone directory.

However you choose your broker, here are some questions to ask:

- How long has the firm been in business?
- How much insurance do they carry to cover the client deposits?
- Who is the insurer?
- What is their schedule of commissions?
- What other service charges apply?
- Are there any *additional* charges?
- What is the investment financial background of the individual who will be handling your account?
- Ask to see a balance sheet and income statement.

Transaction Costs

Though transaction costs for Treasury bills are normally quite low, each broker and bank sets its own rules and these may vary. You will need to know the following:

- How much will you be charged for buying a new issue?
- What is the fee for buying and selling in the open (secondary) market?
- Is there a charge for keeping your Treasury bills in the broker's account?
- Are there other account fees, such as a charge for the monthly statement?
- When do you have to make the payment? (The due date is important.)
- When you sell your Treasury bill, how soon will your cash be available?
- Are there any limitations to your account, such as registration options?

Selling Through a Broker

As stated above, if you sell *before maturity date* you will have to use a broker. A telephone call is all it takes to issue your order to sell your Treasury bill.

Where to Keep
Your Treasury Bills

When you use a broker you have the option of leaving your bills on deposit with your brokerage firm. Although there may be a small charge for this service, many investors find that the convenience is worth the small cost.

Your broker will maintain an account record for your Treasury bills (and any other investments he handles for you) and provide you with a monthly and year-end statement.

You may also choose to take delivery of the securities and store them in a safe location, such as a bank vault. However, the securities must be filed carefully so that they can be retrieved quickly when the bills are to be sold or redeemed. If you use a brokerage firm for acquiring Treasury bills, be sure to discuss the implication of different options with your broker.

It's a good idea when you make your initial contact or your purchase to discuss the ramifications of your broker holding your Treasury bills and other securities for you.

Mutual Funds Specializing in Treasury Securities

What Is a Mutual Fund?

A mutual fund is like a car pool. Many investors ride in the same vehicle to make getting to the destination of their investment goals easier and more convenient. Although there are charges for participating in mutual funds, the price of admission to the club is lower than buying Treasury bills direct from the U.S. Government. Typically, $1,000 is the minimum investment in a mutual fund, and although some funds require a minimum of as much as $25,000, others require no minimum at all.

Because they pool the money of many investors, mutual funds have "market clout" and can provide the same level of professional management for the investor with only $1,000 to invest as one with $1 million or more.

Mutual funds are of interest to the individual investor because they bring a wide variety of investments within reach of smaller amounts of capital. Especially is this the case with Treasury bills, where the initial investment for buying direct from the U.S. Treasury is $10,000.

History of Mutual Funds

Mutual funds have been around since the 1970s. They were designed to specialize in investment management and services. Thus, with a single purchase, the investor has the advantage of professionals making decisions for him or her.

Later on, the fund industry decided to create a group of funds that invest *only* in U.S. Government securities (Treasury bills, notes, and bonds).

In recent years, in response to investors seeking high yields and liquidity, money market funds have flourished. With their substantial pools of assets, these funds are able to invest in securities that are beyond the reach of many individual investors.

Why Mutual Funds Specialize in Treasury Bills

Funds specializing in Treasury bills are short-term funds. Some are called "short-term," others, which may include other Treasury securities beside bills, are called "intermediate-term." In contrast to common stocks, these fixed income securities (such as money market short-term government securities) carry limited risks over the short term.

These funds are based on the belief that the soundest place for an investor's money over the short term is in their professionally managed investments in U.S. Treasury securities. This is due to the purpose and nature of these instruments. With these investments, the investor is *loaning* money to the government in return for the interest to be paid. These "debt securities," unlike stocks, do not represent ownership in a company (or in the government) and their value is therefore "fixed," and cannot increase over time as can stocks in a company. Thus, these funds invest for maximum safety only in short-term, income-producing investments.

Investing in Treasury Bills Via Mutual Funds

Short-term money market portfolios might be termed the "in-between" investment. They are designed to keep your capital working for you between other investments or major financial commitments.

While safeguarding your principal, you earn money market rates on your cash when you invest through a fund, and you enjoy the conveniences and benefits of a professionally managed portfolio.

These portfolios have as their primary objective the attainment of as high a level of current income as is consistent with the safety of capital and liquidity. The funds invest in high-quality, short-term obligations *backed by the full faith and credit of the U.S. Government.* This is a conservative approach and confers a high degree of liquidity.

Although individual funds will differ in the services they make available to their investors, following is a listing of some typical services. When investigating a fund for yourself, you can use this as a checklist:

• **Check Redemption Privilege.** Most funds allow the investor to write checks on the amount of his or her investment, usually in the amount of $500 or more. They often provide personalized checks and always provide you with a detailed statement of the activity in your account.

• **Cash Performance Account.** Most funds combine the service and convenience of a checking account with the earning power of a money market fund. Yields are usually competitive and are readily accessible by check writing. Monthly statements provide detailed account activity and performance. Checks are listed by payee and coded to simplify your tax preparation.

There may be a minimum investment to qualify for this service and an annual charge for it.

• **Immediate Liquidity.** Ordinarily, you can redeem your money at any time by calling the fund or your broker. (There are exceptions and restrictions in some funds.) Usually, the fund will bank wire or otherwise transfer your money the same day as you request the transaction. Usually, there are no penalties or early withdrawal fees

• **Automatic Withdrawal Plan.** Accounts can be set up to receive interest on a regular schedule. (A minimum balance may be required for this service.)

• **Transfer of Funds.** If your investment goals change, you normally can transfer funds in your money market account to another portfolio handled by the same fund.

• **Balance and Yield Information.** Some funds allow you to keep in touch with your investment 24 hours a day through an 800 number.

• **Personal Assistance.** Assistance with your account is available through the fund's investor service during regular business hours.

Investing in mutual funds is simplicity itself. The fund will send you its prospectus on request, along with other vital information and an application form. All you have to do is fill in the form and mail it, along with your check in the amount of your initial invest-ment. The fund will do the rest. Subsequent investments may be made by check or bank wire at any time.

Brokerage clients can simply telephone their brokers and instruct them to carry out the transaction.

One thing to remember: in any money market fund, the yields can move up or down at any time, and there is no assurance that the share price will be maintained, but funds manage their portfolios with the aim of holding the price of the share stable, typically at $1.00 per share.

Important to know, also, is that even though funds invest in U.S. Government securities *only*, they are *not* FDIC insured or government guaranteed, but you can be comfortable in knowing that the fund's portfolio is invested in securities that are backed by the full faith and credit of the U.S. Government.

A Word About Taxes on Fund Yields

Because mutual funds invest in Treasury securities, a substantial portion of the income may be free of state and local income taxes under current regulations. However, we recommend that you talk to your tax advisor or accountant for information on your individual situation. Taxable income from fund yields is reported on your federal income tax return like any other taxable income.

Fund Charges

What Does a Fund Cost?

Costs for investing in a mutual fund fall into two broad categories. One is sales (or redemption) fees; the other is operating expenses.

However, some funds specializing in Treasury securities charge no sales fee. This information is available from the fund's prospectus, which must list costs. If such a fee is applicable, the money usually goes to pay commissions to brokers, financial planners, or others who are involved in selling the fund. No matter who is getting the sales commission, the charge does not relate to the fund's performance, neither helping nor hurting. What the charge does do is affect the amount of money you have to invest. On short-term funds, such as those discussed in this chapter, the fees may be almost negligible.

Although some funds do not charge a redemption fee, all do charge a fee for operating expenses. (They have to make money somehow!) These fees are figured as a percentage of the assets in the fund. If their expense ratio is, for example, 1.25 percent, then the fund claims 1.25 percent of the assets annually as its expense fee.

The expense ratio for the most recent year and for past years is listed in the fund's prospectus. Logically, the more the fund charges to pay its expenses, the less return you will get on your investment. Funds specializing in short-term U.S. Treasuries tend to be low-expense funds. But, if fund charges are important to you (and you should always be aware of what they are), check around. If you are choosing between funds that seem to be equally matched on other points, the lower expense of one may be the tie-breaker.

In any case, what matters is the *net* return on your investment, not how much the fund charges for its services.

Money Market Funds

Latest 30-day Yield is interest earned by the fund for the most recent 30 days and stated at an annual rate. **Days Avg. Maturity** is the average maturity of securities held by the fund. The longer the maturity, the slower the yield will change.

Top-Yielding Money Market Mutual Funds

Name & Telephone Number	30-Day Yield (as of 4/92)	Minimum Required	Days Avg. Maturity
1. United Services Govt. Savings* 800-873-8637	4.59	$ 1,000	31
2. Olde Premium Plus MM* 800-225-3863	4.34	25,000	85
3. Blanchard 100% Treasury* 800-922-7771	4.27	1,000	75
4. Fidelity Spartan* 800-544-8888	4.27	20,000	57
5. Fidelity Spartan US Govt.* 800-544-8888	4.20	20,000	61

6. Riverside Capital*†			
800-752-1823	4.19	1,000	23
7. Alger MM Portfolio*			
800-992-3863	4.16	None	71
8. Mariner Government*			
800-421-8878	4.14	1,000	61
9. Starburst MMF Shares*†			
205-933-4965	4.13	15,000	65
10. Evergreen MM Trust*			
800-235-0064	4.09	2,000	79
National Average	**3.69**		

*Fund is waiving or absorbing all or a portion of the fund's expenses.
Fund is not available in all states.
SOURCE: IBC/Donoghue's Money Fund Report, 290 Eliot St., Box 91004, Ashland, MA. 01721; 800-343-5413

Where to Get Additional Information

To obtain a free prospectus with complete information, which includes management, distribution, and other fees and expenses, just telephone the funds that interest you. They will promptly send you the requested information and will be glad to answer any questions that might arise after you have studied their prospéctuses. Listed below are several other major funds that invest in U.S. Treasuries, along with their telephone numbers:

Carnegie Government Securities Trust
    800-321-2322
Dreyfus 100% U.S. Treasury Money Market Fund, L.P.
    800-782-6620
Fund for Government Investors, Inc.
    800-336-3063
GIT Government Investors Trust
    800-336-3063

Kemper U.S. Government Securities Fund
800-621-1048
Prudential Government Securities Trust
800-642-3503
The Reserve Fund U.S. Treasury Portfolio
800-223-5547
T. Rowe Price U.S. Treasury Funds
800-638-5660
Twentieth Century U.S. Governments
800-345-2021
Vanguard U.S. Treasury Portfolio
800-662-7447
Zweig Government Securities. Series and Money Market Series
800-272-2700

EIGHT

History of the U.S. Treasury and the Federal Reserve

The United States Department of the Treasury, which is an executive department of the Federal government, was established in 1789 by an act of Congress. Its purpose was the collection of taxes, the responsibility for Federal funds, and the keeping of accounts. The first Secretary of the Treasury was Alexander Hamilton.

In the ensuing years since the original mandate, the functions of the Department of the Treasury have been considerably broadened to include affairs not directly related to finance, such as involvement in the banning of the transportation of illegal alcohol during Prohibition and weapons control.

The precursor of the Federal Reserve System was the **Bank of the United States,** established in 1791 by Alexander Hamilton's Federalist party against the opposition of the Jeffersonian party. However, its conservative policies proved unpopular and after the War of 1812 and ensuing financial difficulties, it suffered its demise in 1811 when its charter was not renewed.

In 1812, a second Bank of the United States was chartered for a 20-year period. Monroe appointed Nicolas Biddle as one of its directors and in 1822 he was elected its president. Under his supervision, the bank prospered. But it was viewed skeptically by followers of Andrew Jackson, who thought it a tool of the moneyed class of the Eastern seaboard states. Biddle became the center of an attack against the bank by Jackson, which was a major issue in Jackson's reelection campaign in 1832.

Jackson, victorious, overthrew the bank by vetoing its charter, withdrawing government funds from deposit, and transferring them to state banks (1833). But the Panic of 1837, which was in part a result of the transfer, revealed the fatal flaws of that idea.

Martin van Buren, Jackson's successor, wanted to establish an independent Treasury system isolated from all banks. His efforts were crowned with success in 1840, when a law was passed to this effect, but the victory was overturned by the Whigs, who repealed the law after coming to power in 1841.

President John Tyler (1841–1845) objected to the establishment of another Bank of the United States on constitutional grounds.

Following the Democrats' return to power, an act of August 1846 established the Independent Treasury System. Under this law, public funds were to be kept in coin in the Treasury building and in subtreasuries in various cities. This specie was to be paid out only on proper authority. Bank notes were not considered tender for payments to the Government. The purpose of all this was to make the Treasury independent of the nation's banking and financial system.

However, theory and practice were at variance with each other, and when the Civil War put a strain on the Treasury it became clear that an interdependence between the Treasury and the banking system was necessary.

Although in practice the idea of an independent Treasury had been abandoned by 1898, it remained for the Federal Reserve Act of 1913 to mark the official demise of the old system.

The Federal Reserve System, today the central banking system of the United States, was established by law in 1913. At the time, each of twelve reserve banks (Boston, New York, Philadelphia, Cleveland, Richmond, Atlanta, Chicago, St. Louis, Minneapolis, Kansas City, Dallas, San Francisco) served a national region. Today, there are thirty-five Federal Reserve banks across the country.

In addition to the Federal Reserve Banks, all national banks belong to the system. They must maintain reserves on deposit with their regional Federal Reserve Bank. The system operates on a nonprofit basis, seeking to maintain sound national monetary and credit conditions. It has proved to be a major improvement for American banking.